The repossession of

RILEY

the puppy

The repossession of RILEY the puppy

written by
edward burrell

ISBN 978-1-937550-02-8

Illustrations and cover design by Lance Finley, Firehouse Design LLC
Typeset by Keata Brewer, E.T. Lowe Publishing Company

ACKNOWLEDGEMENTS

I would like to recognize and thank my close friend and illustrator Lance Finley, principal at Firehouse Design LLC, for his creative genius and generosity in sharing it with me.

I would like to thank my friends Beverly Watkins and Sally Sawyer for their input and encouragement and for sharing their vast knowledge of the children's education process with me.

I would like to thank my friend Stephanie Kirby for her editing and organization efforts during the formulation phase of the book. She is extremely smart and a terrific sounding board.

I would like to thank the following friends and their children for their input and encouragement:

Emily Sharpe, home school teacher and mother of Weston Sharpe (age 13), Keaton Sharpe (age 11), and Maddox Sharpe (age 6); three of the smartest children I know.

Laura Street, attorney and mother of Maggie (age 8) and Sam (age 3).

Keata Brewer, book publishing professional and mother of Rossell Brewer (age 13).

I also want to thank my son, Edward, for his encouragement and input, and for making me read "Frosty the Snowman" to him at least six times a night before bedtime when he was a little boy.

Finally, I would like to thank my editor Brittany Sky, professional writer and children's book editor, for her input and final copy edit of the book.

INTRODUCTION
for Moms & Dads

On average, Americans save less and borrow more than most people in the world's industrialized nations. As a consequence of this behavior, the average American family has little or no savings and carries a huge burden of personal debt. It is past time to change these circumstances, and there is no more important place to start than with our children.

Basic math survival skills and the dangers of credit and poor spending habits must be taught to our children. We need to provide them with the skills necessary for financial success and security. We must also help them recognize the consequences of instant gratification from purchasing items without the ability to pay for them before the allure of credit cards tempts them with a perception of trouble-free and limitless money.

I have served in many capacities with financial responsibilities, including that of a financial professional, public accountant, corporate executive, small business owner, father and military officer. After a couple of years in the workforce, I realized that very few are taught how to make good financial decisions. Most people realize they should save some money, but beyond this basic awareness they seldom have the know-how, discipline or skills to save money or make sound financial decisions. It is not how much money your make, but how much you keep.

This book is a shorthand compilation of some of the best financial practices I have found concerning money management. In the book I teach how to save money through the basic concept of financial efficiency and making good choices. I know and understand what must be done to improve your financial circumstances and, if you will allow me, I hope to plant some seeds of success in the minds of your children. My goal with this book is to communicate sound financial principles in such a way that even small children will begin to understand them.

Meet the Logan Family

Mr. and
Mrs. Logan

Gracie
and Jake

Mrs. Logan had taken Gracie and Jake to the mall for some back-to-school shopping. On the way out of the mall, Gracie and Jake begged Mrs. Logan to go to the pet store. Mrs. Logan agreed. While in the store, they found a cute puppy. "Mom, can we please buy this puppy?" the children asked. Mrs. Logan responded with sadness in her eyes, "I'm sorry children; I know you want that puppy, but I don't have the money to buy him." Gracie and Jake became very upset! They began to scream and pitch a fit while Mrs. Logan pleaded with them to stop.

The kids wouldn't give up. They just got louder and louder saying, "We want this puppy! We want this puppy!" Mrs. Logan was very distressed and embarrassed by the behavior of her children.

Mrs. Logan felt pressured into a bad decision just so she could end the embarrassing scene caused by her children's bad behavior. She said to the children, "Okay! Okay! I will buy the puppy, but I must borrow the $300 it costs to get the puppy with a credit card." At that moment Mrs. Logan's heart sank because she knew she would not have the ability to pay the borrowed $300 back.

The family was very excited as they drove home with their cute new puppy. Gracie and Jake discussed many names. Finally, Gracie announced, "Mom, Jake and I have decided to name our new puppy Riley."

Gracie and Jake played in the yard with Riley every day. Riley quickly became an important part of the Logan family. The children loved Riley.

The Logan children were happy because they had gotten Riley, but their mom and dad were not happy because they were in a financial mess. Their bills piled up because they could not pay back the money they borrowed on credit cards. Mr. and Mrs. Logan often sat around late at night and worried about all the money they owed. They recognized they were in big trouble and that it was time to get help managing their money.

At work, Mr. Logan asked his smart and financially successful friend Mr. Watkins for help. "Mr. Watkins, I need some help learning how to manage money," pleaded Mr. Logan. Mr. Watkins said, "Sure, that's easy! You need a copy of *Financial Kamikaze*. It's a finance book that teaches important rules for money management. It explains in simple terms the actions you must take to save money." Mr. Logan thanked him for the information, then went straight to his computer and ordered a copy of *Financial Kamikaze*.

Unfortunately, the Logans were out of time to pay the $300 bill for Riley, their cute new puppy. The very next day, Mrs. Logan got a knock on the door. A man from the pet store credit repossession department demanded to get Riley back because the credit payment was past due. As the man dragged Riley off in a big net, Mrs. Logan pleaded with him, "Please sir, don't take our puppy away. My children will be heartbroken!" The man replied, "I'm sorry lady; I'm just doing my job. You didn't pay your credit card bill on time so the pet store has the right to take their puppy back."

Meanwhile, Gracie and Jake were on their way home from school. As they pulled up to their house, they saw Riley being put in the pet store repossession truck. The truck drove away as they jumped off the school bus. They chased after the pet store truck yelling, "Riley, come back! Riley, come back!"

As the truck drove away, Gracie and Jake cried, "Riley, come back! Riley, come back! Oh, no! Boo hoo hoo! Boo hoo hoo!"

As the truck disappeared down the street, Gracie and Jake continued to cry. "Oh, no! Riley is gone! What are we going to do? What can we do?" The children wondered what happened to their cute puppy Riley.

The kids ran into their house yelling, "Mom! Come quickly! Somebody has taken Riley away in a truck! Why did they take Riley?" Their mother was very upset and crying. "Riley was repossessed by the pet store because I borrowed the $300 to buy him with a credit card. When it was time to pay the money back, I did not have the money to pay the pet store," she explained as she cried.

Later that day, when Mr. Logan got home from work, he called everyone to a family meeting. He wanted to talk about what happened to Riley and the family's difficult financial problem. At the meeting, Mrs. Logan spoke first and explained, "Buying stuff with credit cards got our family in money trouble. Our money problem is the reason why Riley was repossessed by the pet store. Repossession is when the store takes back what you have purchased because you did not pay the money back on time."

Mr. Logan continued, "Buying stuff with a credit card is a promise to pay money in the future. Plus you have to pay extra money called interest just for using credit to buy things. Interest is a terrible thing for families that buy on credit because it makes the money they have to pay back grow bigger faster. When the time came for us to pay the bill for Riley, we did not have the money because we have been spending more money than we earn."

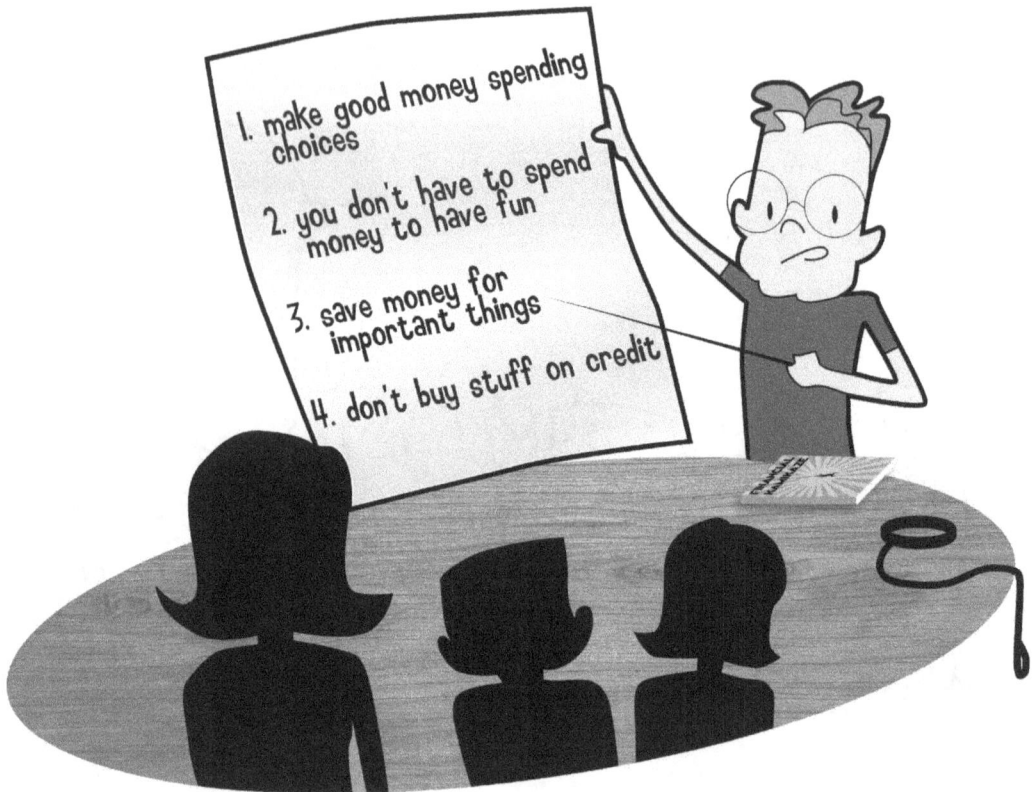

The family continued to talk about the money situation. They came up with a game plan to get Riley back. The parents taught Jake and Gracie the smart money rules they learned about family finances from their new book, *Financial Kamikaze*:

1. Make good money spending choices.
2. You don't have to spend money to have fun.
3. Save money for important things.
4. Don't buy stuff on credit.

Mrs. Logan got out a big empty jar and told the family, "This is where we will keep our money to buy Riley back." She drew progress lines on the big jar and gave it to Gracie and Jake to keep track of their contributions.

The children ran to their bedroom and searched for money. When they found any, they put it in the money jar.

That night, after they put on their pajamas, Jake and Gracie prayed they could find a way to get Riley back. After their prayer, the kids talked about things they could do to save money for Riley's return.

The next day after school, Gracie and Jake heard the music from
the ice cream truck. They both chased the truck down the street to
buy ice cream. They used money they were supposed to be saving
to get Riley back to purchase the ice cream.

When Gracie and Jake got home from the ice cream truck, Mrs. Logan checked the money jar. She discovered some of the saved money was missing. She was upset and very disappointed. She asked her children, "Do you remember the rules your dad and I taught you from our new money book? In order to save money, you must stop purchasing things you don't really need. Only then will you have money for things that are truly important."

Unfortunately, neither Jake nor Gracie learned this important lesson. They continued to buy more junk until they had spent nearly all of their money. Mr. Logan reminded the kids about the smart money rules from his new financial book. "Children, saving money is very important. You must learn to save at least 10 percent of all the money you make. That means for every $10 you have, you should save $1. This is possible when you make good money spending choices." Mr. Logan added, "If we had been saving 10 percent of our money all along, we would already have enough money to buy Riley back."

After hearing his dad talk about making good spending choices, Jake came up with a money-saving idea all by himself! He presented the plan to his mom, dad, and sister Gracie. He said, "We can save a lot of money by making family meals of homemade tuna fish sandwiches instead of spending money on our regular trips to eat at restaurants."

Jake showed his family an old restaurant receipt for $37.78. He explained, "It only costs $5.36 to make tuna fish sandwiches at home. The savings would be a lot—an amazing $32.42!" He concluded, "An average family restaurant meal costs us seven times more money than eating tuna at home!" Everybody liked his plan to save money and agreed to follow it. Mrs. Logan said to Jake, "Jake, this is a very smart plan and a great way to save enough money to buy Riley back." Gracie cheerfully agreed to help Jake make the sandwiches.

On Friday night, instead of going out to eat at their favorite restaurant, Gracie and Jake made tuna fish sandwiches and the family ate an enjoyable—yet inexpensive—meal at home. The money saved went in the jar for Riley.

Later that week, the Logans went to the grocery store. Gracie wanted to buy a drink from the soda machine, but a smart, popular cheerleader from the local high school stopped her and said, "Gracie, if you buy a six-pack of soda, it costs only 40¢ a drink rather than the dollar just one soda costs at the machine. That's a savings of 60¢ a can. You can get twice as many sodas for less money!" Gracie thanked the friendly cheerleader for the good advice and quickly put her money back in her pocket. She asked her mom to buy a six-pack of soda instead. Mrs. Logan bought the six-pack of soda, and they put the money saved in the jar for Riley.

On Saturday, Gracie told Jake and her parents, "I have an idea that will save money and will be fun at the same time. We can skip taking an expensive trip to the movies this afternoon. Instead, we can go on a nature walk at the state park. It will cost practically nothing!" Everybody was excited by Gracie's idea! They couldn't wait to have fun and save money at the same time.

Early that afternoon, the Logans drove to the state park for their
nature walk. While on the walk, the Logan family discovered
all kinds of fun things to do. First, they fed the ducks near the
pond. The baby ducks came right up to them and pecked at the
breadcrumbs. They were very cute.

On the backside of the pond, they found a shallow stream where the kids played in the water. They used fishing nets to catch some minnows. While catching the minnows, they spotted a momma deer with her baby fawn.

When they got hungry, they hiked over to the park's picnic benches. Mrs. Logan unpacked a picnic lunch with their new favorite meal—tuna sandwiches. Everybody had a great time! The money they had saved went straight into the jar for the return of Riley. In the middle of the fun, Jake and Gracie realized that saving money can be easy once you learn how.

The following week, the county fair arrived in town. Grandma Logan came for a visit so she could take Gracie and Jake to the fair. At the fair, she offered to buy the children balloons. They begged her to let them save the money for their puppy Riley instead. They told their Grandma all that they had been learning about saving money, and how bad it is to buy things with credit cards. They told Grandma what had happened to their puppy, Riley. Grandma Logan was surprised to hear Gracie and Jake had become so smart about managing their money. She was even more surprised at their willingness to skip an opportunity to buy balloons. She was very proud of them and agreed, "Alright, children, we can save the money for Riley."

Gracie asked her mom to take them to the pet store. She and Jake were afraid Riley would be resold to another family before they had the $300 they needed to buy him back. At the store, they begged the pet store manager saying, "Please don't sell Riley to anybody else! We plan to buy Riley back. We have $270 and we will soon have $300." The pet store manager replied, "Paying with cash is 10 percent cheaper. So it will cost $30 less. That means your $270 cash will be enough."

Gracie and Jake couldn't believe the good news! They already had
enough money to buy Riley back. The kids rushed home with their
mom so they could get their money jar. They quickly returned
to the pet store to buy Riley back. Mrs. Logan and the children
proudly brought Riley home. Everyone was glad to have him back.

When Mr. Logan arrived home from work, everybody celebrated the return of Riley. They talked about the important lessons they all learned, especially Gracie and Jake.

Gracie told the family what she had learned. "I have learned it is easy to save money once you make saving money important and start making good spending choices." She continued, "I have also learned that we don't have to spend money to have a good time. Remember how much fun we had at the state park?" Everybody agreed and said they remembered.

Jake said, "I have learned that you should never buy things you do not have the money to pay for. The most important lesson for me was learning not to waste money on small things that I really don't need. Then, I will have money I need to buy things that are truly important to me." Both Gracie and Jake learned that buying stuff with a credit card means you are making a promise to pay money in the future and not paying that money back on time could cause great harm.

At that moment, Jake looked down to see Riley chewing on his mother's credit card. He yelled, "Look Mom and Dad, even Riley has something to say about credit cards! I'd say he doesn't like them very much." They all had a good laugh.

Mrs. Logan said to her family, "That's very good, children. I am really proud of what you've done to get Riley back. Now let's make a promise to each other: to never buy anything on credit, to always make good spending choices, and to save at least 10 percent of the money that we earn." Mr. Logan added, "Always remember, we don't have to spend money to have fun."

9 781937 550028